T0208553

COSMO
CONNECTIONS

C I N D Y

BALBOA.
PRESS

A DIVISION OF HAY HOUSE

Scripture taken from the King James Version of the Bible.

Balboa Press books may be ordered through booksellers or by contacting:

Balboa Press
A Division of Hay House
1663 Liberty Drive
Bloomington, IN 47403
www.balboapress.com
1 (877) 407-4847

Because of the dynamic nature of the Internet, any web addresses or links contained in this book may have changed since publication and may no longer be valid. The views expressed in this work are solely those of the author and do not necessarily reflect the views of the publisher, and the publisher hereby disclaims any responsibility for them.

The author of this book does not dispense medical advice or prescribe the use of any technique as a form of treatment for physical, emotional, or medical problems without the advice of a physician, either directly or indirectly. The intent of the author is only to offer information of a general nature to help you in your quest for emotional and spiritual well-being. In the event you use any of the information in this book for yourself, which is your constitutional right, the author and the publisher assume no responsibility for your actions.

Any people depicted in stock imagery provided by Getty Images are models, and such images are being used for illustrative purposes only. Certain stock imagery © Getty Images.

Print information available on the last page.

ISBN: 978-1-9822-0631-4 (sc)
ISBN: 978-1-9822-0633-8 (hc)
ISBN: 978-1-9822-0632-1 (e)

Library of Congress Control Number: 2018907066

Balboa Press rev. date: 06/14/2018

To all there is and all there will ever be.
Cosmo universe having a human experience!

About the Author

"When I started writing in 2005, I trashed it because I was mad at the Lord. My book is inspired by a true story from when I was nine years old until thirty-nine. Now that I think about it, it took Jesus thirty years before walking in his ministry. He was thirty years old. I am glad God did not cast me out! I was hardheaded, stubborn, reckless, and angry—from when I was nine years old until adult age. I knew I was different, so I hid from the world most of the time. When I did go outside, I was not living in my truth. I did not like the poverty-stricken land and knew there was a piece missing from my life; I wanted to go back home to be with the Lord."

Cindy was born in a neighborhood of crackheads and drug dealers. She hated living here on earth. She was not aware of her healing abilities, messages from dreams, and visions because she was focusing on the outside world. Instead of changing the world, her anger drew her environment within herself, bringing more problems into her life. She was afraid of herself and the world, so she became lost. She started drinking alcohol, and her relationships reflected her pain and inner desire. She married a karmic mate. She came to a dead end, writing a suicide note to her family as she attempted to take her life. After going through the dark night of the soul and then enlightenment, her twin flame showed up with the divine, shifting her back to walk the path of healing planet Earth.

CHAPTER

1

Breathe

I WAS TWENTY-SEVEN YEARS old when I stood in the middle hallway of my two-bedroom apartment in Maryland. I went to the bathroom medicine cabinet and grabbed a bottle full of pills. I was in the process of writing my suicide note to my family, explaining how sorry I was for exiting the earth to be back with the Lord. After running around in the wilderness, I was getting tired of the land. I tried everything from sex and alcohol to marriage. Nothing seemed to fill the emptiness I was feeling. I was a divorced mother of four children who was trying to find a fit in life. I looked at the pills and filled my hand with all of them. But then I heard a voice telling me to breathe! I felt a blanket come over me as I fell unconscious onto my bed.

CHAPTER

2

Childhood

WHEN I WAS NINE years old, I was in a state of despair. I was disgusted with my life. I hadn't lived that long and hadn't had a chance to experience enough to be dissatisfied with my life. Well, let's just say that I was angry! I was tired of the birds flying through our kitchen vent, the mice climbing up the sheets in broad daylight, and people killing each other in the apartment building because of bad drug deals.

I was born and raised in Maryland. My mom and dad loved each other dearly, but they always seemed to be fighting. Enough was enough for me! I marched right into my mom's room and said, "I hate it here on earth."

"Good," she replied. "Why don't you tell God, and maybe he will take you out."

I walked away in fear, yet I was sad at the same time. I didn't understand how we could have such a loving God with people suffering on earth. At a very young age, I believed in God and magic. I didn't understand what I was missing from my life, but I felt I belonged in a faraway place, and I longed to be there again.

CHAPTER

3

Hold On

I WAS SIXTEEN YEARS old when I had my daughter. I knew she would fulfill the emptiness of my heart. Just as I was lying on the bed at the hospital, I waited for them to deliver her to my room. Instead, the nurse and the doctor walked in, dismayed. "Your daughter seems to be doing well," the doctor said.

Then silence!

My heart started racing. He continued. "She has a gap between her vagina that seems to develop a male hormone in the form of a penis. This is an unusual circumstance, and with this type of problem, two things will happen. Within three days, the vagina that was not formed properly in the womb will start to form, or she will die."

I could not hear anything else that came out of his mouth, as he was still uttering his words. I was fainting because I didn't understand. I was already sad. I sat in silence with tears running down my face. They proceeded to walk out of the room, and I felt like they were ghosts who had come to deliver a message.

Three days later, the doctor walked into the room with a half smile. "Your healthy baby girl will be in shortly," he said.

I started to feel okay living on earth. I was engaged to her handsome father. We had our ups and downs, but this man loved the Lord. We had conversations about growing old together. We loved watching the movie *Ghost,* which featured Whoopi Goldberg. He even told me that we would always be together and that when he died, he was going to visit me. It made me feel uncomfortable. "We all will die someday," he said.

I was driving my car down the highway. I saw a vision of my car hitting a pole and blowing up. It happened two more times on different days. I thought, *If I am going to die, I have to tell my family. Wait. I am not ready to die.*

"Lord, I'm sorry. I know I wanted to die when I was young, but I am okay now," I said.

I went home to lie on my bed. I was single and separated from my daughter's father at the time. So I decided to watch the movie *Two Can Play That Game,* featuring Vivica Fox and Morris Chestnut. Morris Chestnut reminded me of him because they had similar features. My ex had those football-looking shoulders. He was around six foot one and weighed 140 pounds. He had brown skin that would smooth over any woman.

CHAPTER

4

When Death Calls

IN THE MIDDLE OF enjoying my movie, my mom called me a few times, but I ignored her. Finally, she left a voice message. "Call me back as soon as possible. Your daughter's father died in a car accident."

Was she saying this to get me to call her back? But she never lied to me, and this was not a joke. I phoned her.

"Hello. He died in a fatal car accident," she said.

I could not utter a hello, and no words would come out of my mouth. Finally, with shaking lips, I said, "I don't understand."

"Everything happens for a reason," she said.

It was not just his death that made me weep but the sadness of living on earth with emptiness.

"Go calm yourself down, and we'll talk later," she said.

I balled myself up in the fetal position with the blanket wrapped around me like a mother would cuddle her baby. I did not want to have a conversation with the Lord because he seemed not to be listening anyway. It was around ten o'clock that night. I could not sleep. I thought, *Where did he go? I did not say goodbye.*

I was all cried out and only felt my heart aching. I heard wind coming from my window, but it was not windy outside. I knew I was being selfish and did not understand why the Lord took him. He loved the Lord.

But who was the Lord?

"I want him back," I said. "Bring him back!"

I heard footsteps in my room and did not know why because no one else was there. I hid my face under the covers. *Am I going crazy?* Then a bright light from my distant bathroom shined through my room. I pulled down my covers, and he was standing there in the middle of my floor.

I covered my eyes because his spirit was too bright, and it scared me to death. I felt like I was going to meet him on the other side because my heart was pumping out of my chest. I got in my car and jetted!

As I drove to my mom's house, I could feel him sitting in the back seat of my car. I was glad I did not see him because I did not want to get into a car accident.

I pulled up at my mom's house and banged hard on her front door.

"What is wrong with you, girl?" she said.

"I saw him!"

"What are you talking about? Maybe you're tired and need rest. Come on in and get some sleep."

As I was walking up the stairs, I could hear footsteps behind me. I said, "What is it? Why are you following me?" I was having a conversation with the dead. I knew I was losing my mind!

That was when I remembered our conversation about the movie *Ghost*. He had to tell me something. I lay on the bottom bunk bed my mom had in one of the rooms. I could hear him walk around. I wrapped myself tight under the covers. I didn't want to listen. I was so afraid as I drifted off to sleep.

I met him standing in my dream. He looked at me and said, "Do you forgive me?"

Then I saw another bright light behind me. That was the Lord! I wanted to meet him, but the look on his face was not an exciting one. I felt sad because I couldn't move in my dream. I couldn't turn around. I looked at him and said, "Did you know you were a good man? Did you know that?"

He gave me a hug and a smile and then disappeared!

In the morning, I went to my mom and told her what had happened. She confirmed that he had also visited his family. I was hoping it all was a dream when I woke up. But I was at peace.

I still think about him today, and I cry. I will forever feel his spirit!

CHAPTER

5

My Soul Friends

I KNEW I HAD to accept his death because I already had a new baby girl by another soul mate. He was loving and showed me so much love, and I was not ready. I met him at a warehouse. He was my lover. We spent five years together on and off. I also noticed that I was trying to change who he was. It was something about me that I wanted to change. I did not know how to open up to this kind of love that was standing before me. It was the same love I had in myself, and it reflected the need for change on the outside.

When I emerged into such a great moment, I started to have unconditional love for people around me. However, it was coming out in flirting. I apologized for missing my birth control pills for many nights because I noticed he was not my forever partner. He even told me he was not ready to have a baby. I believe when a man informs us women of this, we should listen and respect the situation by using condoms and other preventive measures. I am very proud I have my daughter, who is an American Indian healer.

I decided to get my life back from men and learn to love and cherish myself. At the age of twenty-five, I decided to go to a club for the first time. I went there feeling like a princess going to find my prince charming. Was I done with men? I had on some apple-bottom jeans, a crop top, and heels. I weighed 120 pounds and stood five foot five. I felt amazing that night. I danced all night with everyone. I was having the time of my life until I saw this gorgeous man who stood six four and weighed about 185. I saw a light shining on him (white light in the club). He seemed to notice me too as he walked over to where I stood. Then he disappeared. Where did he go? He was dancing with a dark-skinned, smooth-toned, small-framed woman. He was in the middle of the floor as he stared right at me. So I decided to dance in front of another guy; I don't recall his face because I was dancing in front of him from behind.

As I turned around, I saw that my handsome guy had moved the other guy out of the way to dance with me. He was my shining armor I had created in my mind before going to the club. I couldn't believe I had envisioned this man into my reality so quickly. I am sure it was a lot of emotions and strong vibrations that drew him toward me (I was not aware of this creation process at the time). I could not understand the intensity of our chemistry together. It was my first experience of a one-night stand. We were walking toward the hotel building. I looked around the corner to make sure no one saw me. It was way out of character for me. Inside the room was my delight. I felt all my desires in the base of my spine.

I also met a black woman who resembled a flawless Native American that same week. She had beautiful dark skin and thin, wavy hair. I saw my reflection within her. I remember taking a shower and crying out to the Lord, "Oh Lord, help me! Deliver me from this, I plead." She came in the bathroom and pulled back the shower curtain. I screamed. "What is wrong with you?" she said. I got out of the shower, finished up what I came to do; sex and left. When I felt more of my female energy and my full masculine side, both of them disappeared from my life.

CHAPTER

6

Wake-up Call

HAVE YOU EVER LOVED someone and hated them just as much? Was it the same dark forces within me? Well, that was my karmic mate. As much as I loved his goofiness, I hated him with fire! The one good thing I recall was the sex, but even after that, I felt disgusted with myself. I felt energy leaving my body. Sometimes I know we are aware of toxic relationships and choose to stay. The marriage had me running, and I got saved and met my Lord, Jesus! It was painful and a blessing, and I had no choice but to run to the light.

I was standing in the courtroom in Maryland, ready to get married at the justice of the peace. A family member stood there as a witness. I can still hear her voice in my head: *"He beat you because he is jealous, and he loves you!"* Sadness welled up in my eyes, the same sadness I remembered as a child. I knew it was not right then—and not right now! It was a voice that called for me to *run!*

I had not forgiven my father for the fights he had with my mother.

It was a deep-rooted pain that transferred as a mirror within my husband. Leaving the altar, I looked up at the sky, wondering, *What have I done now?* I wanted a hug from the Lord himself because no one understood the pain I was feeling. Unresolved issues from when I was a child were still with me at the age of twenty-seven.

As my husband and I entered the home, I tried to shake off the bad vibe that I was feeling. "So, how do we celebrate our honeymoon?" I said.

He was lying in the bed, and he had his back toward me. He turned and faced me and said, "Honeymoon? Ha!" He looked into my eyes. "Welcome to hell," he said. I crunched myself into a fetal position and cried myself to sleep. I knew I was in a situation and needed to reach out for help. I knew he was cheating on me and running all over me because the same angry little girl came out, throwing a shoe at the wall where it missed his face. In returned, I was dragged and slammed to the floor four times. I was five months' pregnant with his son.

Two weeks later, I had severe pain in my abdomen. My mom gave me a heating pad. It did not help. I walked into the hospital and stumbled toward the floor. They admitted me for deep vein thrombosis for thirty days. I could not walk and was on full bedrest, using a bedpan. The blood clot traveled from my abdomen to my left thigh. I leaned toward one side of the bed; the nurse was sliding the bedpan for me to pee. I kept crying as the nurse said, "You will pee soon, and this time will pass and become only a memory." Time passed, and it had been three days without any urine secretion or bowel movement. I lay on my back as the pain traveled down my leg. One thigh was three times bigger than the other. My belly was just as big, and I did not see how the urine was going to flow into a bedpan.

I turned my body on the bed, trying to get everything within me to move around so I could pass my urine.

There was only one thing left to do, imagine. The nurse came back on the fourth day. "Are you ready to go on the bedpan today?" she said. I smiled. It was time to put my imagination to work. As I sat on the bedpan, I closed my eyes to a vision. I could hear my urine dropping in the toilet. That is when I opened my eyes, and my real urine was passing through me. I used the rest of my thirty days in the hospital to heal myself. I knew when I got out, it was time for me to go home and create a new home.

Social services came and asked questions; it was the same protocol and procedure regarding abuse, which I denied. My husband walked in the room. I saw his soul hurting. He kept saying hurtful words to me as he texted another woman. I did not know how I was going to get him and me the help we needed. He sat there crunching on his chips. "Next time, leave me the hell alone," he said. I do not know if he saw himself as needing help or me needing it. I sat quietly and was aware of it all.

CHAPTER

7

Miracles

MY FIRSTBORN SON WAS two years old. I was heading to the hospital to have a procedure, tube ligation. The nurse came in to do the bloodwork and drape me in a gown. The doctor came in and stared at me. My heart started to race because his glare let me know my blood was abnormal. He proceeded to say, "What kind of preventive measures did you use after having your son?"

I became unconscious until the nurse yelled, "Miss!"

Now I could see the doctor's face again, but sweat was dripping off my forehead. The doctor moved in closer, gave me a light tap on the leg, and said, "Congratulations. Everything happens for a reason."

I tried to stay strong as I got up and left to go to my car. I couldn't wait to get home because my bathroom was where the Lord and I would talk. I went to the bathroom and sat on the toilet, and before I started to speak to the Lord, my tears overwhelmed me as my chest rose and fell. I finally came out and said to the Lord that I would not be keeping that unborn child. I went on to pledge to the Lord the reasons why I could not birth another baby.

The bathroom was silent. I wanted an answer before leaving because I would be heading straight to the abortion clinic. I fell to my knees and started to shake in physical and mental pain. My face fell toward the bathroom cold floor. I heard a small voice within my spirit say, "If you abort the baby, you will die during aborting."

I rolled over on my back and stared at the bathroom ceiling. "There must be a reason for all this," I said to the Lord. "Well, fine enough, but I'm going to need your help."

I was working in a doctor's office in 2006. The doctor found out she was in her last stage of cancer, and a week later, she died. It was before I knew I was pregnant with my second son, which was my fourth child. I went on a thirty-day fast. It was my first time; I had just learned about fasting and cleansing. I did not eat until the sun went down. I did not tell my husband that in two more weeks, the office would be closed, and I was now pregnant with his second child. I went home that night to discuss everything with him. "You worthless piece of shit," he said. I started to think to myself, *Am I worthless?*

I was watching TD Jakes on the TV when I heard, "Get up and go." It struck my heart.

I went online to apply for a job.

I came home and told my husband I had an interview. "You will not get that job because you are a dummy," he said.

I smiled and walked away because he was defeated. "No weapon formed against me shall prosper, and every tongue which rises against me in judgment will be condemned, this is the heritage of the servants of the Lord, and their righteousness is of me, says the Lord" (Isaiah 54:17).

Two weeks later, I was working at the hospital in Silver Spring. My actions allowed change to come to me. I remember feeling the Lord's goodness during my interview. It was the easiest one yet. I was sitting at my desk in the neuro intensive care unit when I heard within my spirit that my son would be the holy child out of all my kids. No one would touch the wound. I had to stay free from sex during my pregnancy.

I began looking for an apartment on the internet when my computer kept flicking back to a particular home. I rebooted my computer, and it took me back. There was no way I was going to be able to afford that house with my salary. I was making $10.50 an hour as a unit coordinator. So, I decided to write down the number to phone the Realtor when I got off work. When driving home, I dialed the number and started talking. He didn't give me any details but said to meet him at the house, and he would show me around. He didn't even ask about monthly rent yet or speak about the application process. I pulled up and saw the house, and I knew I was in the wrong neighborhood—until I looked again at the address.

I stepped out of the car and scanned the area. One lady was in her yard, looking peaceful. I knock on the front door and entered the home. The living room had a large window and an electric fireplace. Toward my left was the dining room, bathroom, family area, and bedroom. "Well, miss, how much can you afford?" he said.

I wanted to say it looked too expensive, but a voice within me said, "I could give you eight hundred a month." I verbalized what I felt.

He said, "Fair enough. One side of the house is all yours." It was two bedrooms, a bath, and washer and dryer. It was all I needed.

He also told me he rented out another room to a single mother who had one child. The mortgage was five thousand a month, and he covered the rest of the rent.

I went home to pack my things and looked up the home one more time on the internet. It was a half-million-dollar home. I lay back in my car, and I knew at that very moment I was guided and protected by the Lord. His goodness became so vivid and real I started to shiver.

It was time for the delivery of my son. I was having back pains. I phoned 911, and they said I would be going to another hospital where I resided. I hung up the phone because I wanted to deliver at the hospital where I worked because that was where I felt a flow of blessings and peace. I got in the car to drive myself. It was thirty minutes away. I was scared because I had been having the pain in my back for a while, and I had started to bleed. I wanted someone to go with me, but there was no one home but me. I prayed to the Lord that I would have a safe drive to the hospital. I got in the car. I took a break and slowed down on the highway; the cars were beeping at me. I placed my left arm around my belly as I drove with the other hand.

I parked my car and got out to hold my belly, as if my son was going to fall out. I walked in the hospital sweating, and the nurse came running. "Oh my God, she's about to have a baby," she said. I lay back in the wheelchair as she wheeled me to the delivery floor.

I was glad I was only six centimeters. I was able to get an epidural. The man walked in and touched my back as he numbed it and prepared the needle. It took him an hour. Yes, an hour! He said my spine was crooked. I had three kids, and no such thing had ever been said. I heard the voice of mighty warriors around me. That is when I knew it was my death certification. When I saw big drops of sweat running down my forehead, I saw them beating my Lord on the cross. I heard the doctor say, "I almost have it," with trembling fear, as if he was about to paralyze me. I got even more paranoid. I went back in my vision to focus on my Lord's Crucifixion because it was pain and power.

The nurse reached over to hug me tight from the front as I sat on the bed. She said, "Squeeze my hand as much as you like." I heard her weeping on my chest.

I said within my spirit, "Oh, Jesus, they killed my savior. Look what they did." I felt all the pain in my body.

It was over when the doctor said, "Great. Could you move around for me please?" I moved slowly around and saw the nurse's wet face from my sweaty shirt and her tears. It was drenched in sweat; in my vision, I saw blood. I proceeded to lie on my back and had a full understanding that day of why Jesus went to the cross and how painful his death was.

I lay on my back in the bed in peace. It was my time to catch a break and breathe, until I felt pressure going down my legs. I called out for help, and I could not believe the nurse left me alone. I said, "Hello? Is anywhere here?" I looked around in the room, and everyone was gone. The pressure was between my legs. I opened my legs to give it some relief. There on the edge of the bed, my son was still in his sack like a bubble baby. I laid my head back. There was no need to figure this one out.

The nurse and the doctor came in at the same time. They said, "Perfect timing," until they saw my son on the bed with an unbroken sack. "Oh my goodness!" the doctor yelled.

The nurse smiles and yelled, "Miracle baby!"

The doctor punctured the bag, and my son's lungs started to cry. He was healthy enough, according to the doctor, for my son and me to go home.

Three weeks later, I was at my mom's dining table feeding my son. The milk kept projecting out of his mouth. He looked lean and lifeless. My mom said, "You have to take him in. Maybe they will change his formula." I took him to the pediatrician in Maryland, where I was instructed to take him to the radiology department.

The tech was doing her job when she became silent and then said, "Wow!" She instructed me to take him to the hospital in Washington, DC.

The doctor came into the room and said, "We are keeping your son for an emergency procedure (pyloric stenosis)." I started to panic. I could not breathe. If the Lord wanted me to keep the baby, why was I going through such pain? One day later, they could not do the procedure because his electrolytes were not right to do so. They had to use plenty of IV fluids to get his electrolytes back up because he was starving from birth to three weeks old.

I went back toward the room where he was lying in a covered plastic machine. He was so tiny and fragile. He took his thumb and placed it toward his mouth as if it was his place of comfort. He spent three more weeks without food. Finally, it was his time for surgery. The doctor guided me to the waiting room. I sat in the chair weeping.

I sat for four hours until the doctor came in. I jumped up, hoping no one was going to deliver me more pain. He smiled and said, "You may see your son." I walked toward the back recovery area and felt the pain lifting off my shoulders. I held him in my arms and stared at him. He was my miracle, and I cried on him for his deliverance.

The nurse walked in and said, "Here is his bottle. We left the first feeding for you." My tears were still dropping down my cheeks, and I thanked the Lord for her.

Upon returning to my home, the man who was renting the house decided to ask me for special favors to keep the rent cheap. I said, "No, thank you." That place was a holy place where the Lord had sent me; I knew I was asking for trouble if I did something stupid there. I did not have the desire to. I knew it was my time to exit. The house was to keep me purified during my pregnancy. The Lord was faithful to me, and it was my time to start searching for the meaning of life. I found an apartment in Maryland.

CHAPTER

8

Get Up

I WAS TWENTY-SEVEN YEARS old when I stood in the middle hallway of my two-bedroom apartment. I went into the bathroom medicine cabinet and grabbed a bottle full of pills. I was in the process of writing my suicide note to my family, explaining how sorry I was for exiting earth to be back with the Lord. After running around in the wilderness, I was getting tired of the land. I tried everything from sex, alcohol, and marriage. Nothing seemed to fill the emptiness I was feeling. I was a divorced mother of four children, trying to find a fit in life. I looked at the pills and filled the palm of my hands with all that had been in the bottle. I heard a voice telling me to breathe!

I felt a blanket on me as I went unconscious on my bed, facedown. Some people would call it the Holy Spirit. I knew it was a state of rest. I felt a tear run down my cheek, and my body could not move as I lay on my stomach with both arms resting at my side. A chill of wind went over and through me. After hours of lying there, "Get up," I heard an invisible voice say to me. I knew it was a critical point in my life to make a change. *Where do I begin?* I had four children and was a certified medical assistant.

CHAPTER

9

First Step toward Change

I WAS ONLY MAKING eleven dollars an hour as a medical assistant and went to take an exam to become a certified phlebotomist. I gained employment in a medical lab at another hospital in Clinton, Maryland. My pay went up to $16.20. I was doing okay at the time—or at least I thought I was. It was the first step toward change. However, I still felt different since falling on my face after an attempted suicide. I could feel energy traveling throughout my body as vibration, mostly felt in quiet times and being still. I wanted more for myself (as we always do). So, I started college. My life was under control, and I had everything in order. Or did I?

I was working at the hospital for nine months when my code blue pager went off. Code blue is a cardiac arrest. I felt energy vibrating in my body, and I could not keep still as I stopped in front of the unit on the second floor. The nurse resuscitated the patient, and the doctor was looking down her airway with a scope. "I need a third person to give the other nurse a break from CPR!" the charge nurse yelled. "You! Phlebotomist—come here!" My hands were clammy, and my heart was palpitating. A flow of energy moved gently throughout my body. I placed my hands in the middle of the lady's chest to start chest compressions.

I glanced at the doctor, who was still checking her airway for food particles, and then at the nurse, who stood in front of me with weary eyes, looking as if she had not gotten rest the night before. I felt overwhelmed, and I needed calmness. I closed my eyes and saw the lady's heart in my vision. I didn't know if I should run or not, but I felt peace and serenity where I was standing. I saw her heart in irregular rhythm like quivering Jell-O. I knew it was abnormal, so I changed the rhythm to a steady beat in my mind, continuing the chest compressions. I had forgotten everyone was in the room until the nurse yelled, "Stop! We have a heartbeat."

The doctor looked over the top of his glasses with a curious look. I turned the other way to head toward the trash, where I placed my used gloves. I grabbed my phlebotomist tray and left the room. I walked quickly down the hall, where I was going to cut the corner and run! The nurse ran behind me. "Excuse me" she said. "Hello? You, phlebotomist!" I decided to turn around. "What is your name?"

"Cindy," I replied.

"I haven't seen you around before. Neither have I seen an efficient and effective CPR from a phlebotomist!" She wrote down my badge number and department name.

I went back to my unit. The director approached me. "Do you know what you did to our unit, young lady?" he said. "In all my years of working here, no such recognition has come to my department."

"I did not do it," I said. "It was the Lord!"

"It's okay to give yourself some credit; you took part in the process." He smiled.

It was time for the ceremony. The director headed toward the front to give his speech regarding my moral character. I walked behind him, thinking about what I was going to say. I looked down, and my body was trembling. After he finished his speech, he handed me the mic.

"I was in the room. We, as a team, gave life," I said nervously.

Two weeks later, I was in the hospital newspaper, an article and a picture of me saving a life. I was mad at the Lord. "Why did you do this to me?" I did not like the attention.

Every time I turned the corner in the hospital, they would say, "Here comes the blessed one!" However, I was not blessed. I was living a painful and dreadful life. I was known as a quiet person. I felt alone. I had to spend nights and days alone in my room, drained from the public energy. *What is wrong with me? I can never seem to be comfortable here on earth!*

CHAPTER

10

Dark Night of the Soul

I HAD BEEN WORKING two years at the hospital and had thirty-six college credits. I decided to relocate from Maryland to a different county. There was so much pain in that city for me, and I wanted out! I had a strong desire to start over. But at what cost? When I relocated to a home in Anne Arundel County, I was still attending a community college and working at the hospital.

How would I survive? I set goals for myself, and it did not seem to bring me peace. I remember emailing my college professor during the summer semester, letting him know that I would not be attending his class anymore. "But why?" he said. "You only have two weeks left, and you worked so hard."

A tear rolled down my cheek at the public library as I walked out. I went home and lay quietly in my bed. I whispered to the Lord, "I am still tired, and this emptiness in my heart will not go away."

I heard a whisper in the form of another wind (the same wind that surrounded me during my attempted suicide). "No one, having put his hand to the plow, and looking back, is fit for the kingdom of God" (Luke 9:62).

I placed both hands on my closed eyelids to figure out if I was going to answer the call of the Lord or not. My life was too painful not to. It was even more painful to walk into the unknown. I was going through the dark night of the soul.

I got up to make the call to the hospital, to tell them that I would no longer be working for the department. My hands were clammy and shaking, and I could not help but wonder if I was making the right choice. I knew I had heard from God and that he would be with me through it all. Even if it meant God was paying for my car note and bills after leaving the hospital, right?

Three months later, I woke up and went outside to the parking lot in front of my building, wondering, *Where in the hell is my car?* I was new in the Lord, walking with him, and surely he would not let anyone take my car. I had heard different stories from Christians about how the Lord had paid for their debt. I called the bank where my car was financed. "Someone stole my car," I said.

"Ma'am, your car has been repoed!" As I stood in the middle of the street, I heard those words echoing in my ear. I had dropped out of college and left my job, a mother of four children. No car. I had nothing! The only thing I had left was to go within myself.

Who am I? Why am I here? I curled up in a fetal position on my bed, rocking myself to sleep. Who going to believe that I heard from God (my initiation) or higher self? I could not share this with my family without them calling me nuts. I went back into a state of depression. I was not even hungry. Days went by, and I would forget that I did not eat until my stomach started rumbling. This new energy within my body was sustaining me, but I knew it was time to take care of my physical body as well. Why was I suffering in this world? As I sat in my room, all the pain from childhood, relationships, and divorce started to rise within me. I had buried the pain by always keeping busy. However, now there was nowhere to run.

CHAPTER

11

Awakening

I DID NOT HAVE my brand-new car anymore. My housing, food, children, and mind were sustained, thanks to my family and their loving support. For the first time, I felt my heart open. I started to see flashes in the middle of my forehead. Some people refer to this as the third eye (eye of the soul). I had nothing, and my family bought us food to survive. I was on a soul journey toward *awakening!*

I had to walk in it alone. I didn't want to go outside, and I stayed away from the malls and shopping center for years. I knew something was happening because I would get a glimpse of the fifth-dimension consciousness. I was in a state of peace, joy, and love for everyone, and for once, I could feel the negative thought and perception of the world that I once had being filtered out of my mind. On two occasions, I had an out-of-body experience. I looked down at my form lying on the bed while I was floating in the air. I was at peace and scared at the same time. At that moment, I zapped right back into my body.

I got up to get me and the children ready to go outside to meet my brother to take my kids to my parents' house to stay during the weekdays. It was my first time seeing the light outside for weeks. I remember sleeping or lying in my bed day after day while my body was transforming into a higher vibration. I walked with my head toward the ground in shame because I had nothing. As I glanced up at the sky, I saw three faces in the clouds. It was my first time smiling after years.

I was at my mom's house when my dad let me drive his truck. I went to the dollar store to purchase some items. I remember stepping out and closing the door. Because I had so much on my mind at the time, I left the key inside. As I heard the door lock itself, I noticed the key was still on the seat of the car. I was not going to call my dad and tell him. I was stuck in front of the dollar store looking silly. I was tired of calling for help for people to solve my problems.

In my state of despair, I had not been speaking to the Lord as much. However, that day, if God was real, I needed him to rise! I paced around the truck in circles, saying, "Oh Jesus, my Lord! You are a miracle!" I felt all my emotions and heart racing as tears flowed down my face. I was calling the Lord forward to this present time, moment, and space. I saw the number three as some form of completion, so I paced two more times around the truck. Then I stopped on the driver's side where I felt tingling coming from the inside of the palms of my hands. I touched the door, and all the locks popped open.

I instantly ran from the car. I turned back, slowly moving forward toward the window to make sure Jesus was not sitting in the seat. *I am having a breakdown moment.* I knew God loved me and cared, but I was afraid of myself and everyone else. I was trying to discover what this life was all about—and what I was all about. I got in the car and sat in the driver's seat. I started up the car, and I started to cry as I praised God for helping me.

Two weeks later, my brother dropped the kids and me off at home. I wanted to do some laundry. My mom had given me a washer months ago. I hand-dried the clothes by hanging them up in the closet. That Sunday, I walked downstairs to the half bathroom to start the washing machine. It would not start. I looked at the hand that was tingling when I opened my dad's truck; I noticed it was just a regular hand. *What am I doing? Am I going crazy? Am I nuts to think my hand is a healer?* I went to sleep that night trying to understand the logic behind a broken washing machine. I remembered it in its beautiful state of flowing water, and I chuckled to myself at the beautiful waterfall I saw in my vision as I went to sleep.

When I got up in the morning, the sun was beaming through my window, and I could still see that beautiful water coming from my washing machine. I ran downstairs with a basket full of laundry like an excited, playful child. I touched the start button, and the water started flowing down the washer. I stood there looking at the beauty of it. Then I realized I had done it again! I took a deep breath. *Girl, you are going to have to figure it out. Who the hell are you?*

CHAPTER

12

What Was That?

I WAS IN THE process of transferring my kids from one county to another. They were still in the same county where my mom lived. I would only go home on the weekend. It was in 2010 after leaving the hospital and losing my car. My mom loved to walk up the hill to take the kids to school. I would stay in the house with my niece and nephew, where my mom had a daycare center in her home. Sometimes I would walk with her to take the kids to school. That hill would burn anybody's thighs. It was a good workout.

It was summer. I had the urge to walk and enjoy the weather. In my spare time, I would work out by running three miles straight. However, I would avoid most of the hills. Running became a stress reliever for me. I was separated and planned on getting a divorce soon. I was not in the dating game at the time. It was going on one year without any sexual encounters. It was my four-year-old son's first year in prekindergarten. It was a tough time for me because his father was not around, and I had this beautiful yet dreadful experience by myself. This time, my mom did not walk my son into the classroom. I did.

Before walking into the building, I saw this man who stood six one and weighed around 170. It was not just his physical appearance; there was magnetic pull coming from the source of my spirit.

A bunch of kids were standing around him. He seemed to have all the children drawn to him. He worked in the school, but at the time, I did not know where. I wanted to ask him if he was married, because I couldn't understand what I was feeling inside at the time. So, I did. As I slowly went to approach him, my heart started to race. I stopped and thought over in my mind what I was going to say so I did not embarrass myself.

I stood in the middle of the crowd and stared at him. As he looked my way, I turned my head toward the other direction. I could feel him staring at my back. It was a weird and creepy feeling as my heart continued to pound. A child distracted him, and he continued to speak to them again. I moved toward him slowly. I stood in front of him.

He stared at me, and I stayed there for a second. I thought, *Say something, dummy.* "Excuse me, are you married?"

He said, "Yes, I am."

I started walking backward and said, "I'm sorry." I turned around because I almost ran a little kid over with my nervousness.

It sounded like the guy chuckled. Then he said, "Don't be sorry."

I walked my son into the school building to go to his class. My son was still scared of staying in the school, so he decided to run. Where in the hell was the teacher? I needed someone to help me take him back in. My mom had told me every day about my son running, and it was my chance to experience it for myself.

The teacher popped around the corner. "Hello," she said and introduced herself. "You must be his mom because Grandma always brings him." At that moment, I committed to being more involved in my kid's life, though I seemed to be out in space, searching for answers all the time. I decided to live in the present moment. His teacher said, "No worries. The other teacher is here, and he always takes him to help me in the class and with all the children."

The same man I had approached moved toward the door, and I became frozen again. Time, space, and the world stood still. The teacher smiled and walked away.

I stood there with my son as I moved him toward the teacher. "Okay, I have to go now," I said." My palms were sweating. I had no control of my son running. He was crying, and the teacher took him in the room where they stood behind the see-through glass of the door. I looked down at my son with his tears rolling down his face. My tears dropped. The glance between the teacher and me was locked through the door that held the space between us. What I saw in him was beautiful, and there were all my fears. I saw myself in him. I stepped back as I broke the glance. For the first time, I knew who he was.

He was the one I had been looking for since I was a child.

I dismissed the thought and went back to my mom's house. I ran the track that morning, trying to figure it all out. As I saw his face in my mind, I ran faster and faster. When I slowed down, I told myself I would not go back to that school. But then I remembered my vow to live in the present moment and be there for my son.

The next day, I took my son to his class. I walked fast. I wanted to drop him off and run straight out the back door, avoiding his teacher altogether. I was so glad he was not in the classroom. The other teacher held onto my son to stop him from running. I ran out of the classroom and around the corner. The back door outside gave me my air back. I couldn't believe I had been holding my breath, timing myself to get in and get out of the building. I walked up the sidewalk to get in my car.

"Excuse me," I heard a voice said behind me. Time stood still again. I turned around slowly and was mad at myself for my poor timing. He said, "You don't have to run."

"You are married." I heard my voice trembling.

"There are always friends, right?" he said. I gave him my number, and he typed it into his phone. I walked away, and as I turned around, we met each other's glance again.

One week later, I saw a text on my phone that said, "Hi!" It was almost like I heard the words echo through the phone. His words pierced my heart. It affected me in a way I could not explain.

We met up after his work hours to discuss our situations and all the bad things we had done. We were confessing our sins to one another. I sat and thought, *This is the weirdest thing and situation I've ever encountered.* I felt free for the first time. I sat and stared at him as he was going through his papers on the desk. Someone walked in and asked him a question, and he lost his thoughts for words. I was not the only one having this magical moment or whatever it was. He dropped his papers and proceeded to pick them up. The lady that had walked in looked at me and then looked at him again; she smiled and walked away.

When he finally came close, I said to myself, "It is him!" I could feel the words and the vibration of another magnetic pull. I kept myself calm because I didn't want to be in this situation with a married man. We went outside where we could talk, and three hours passed. I didn't want him to go.

This talking went on for six more months—until one day we stood in the middle of the classroom. All the kids had left for afternoon buses. I had already dropped my son off and had returned to visit the teacher.

We became close friends, and I felt something for him at the same time. I didn't understand what was going on in the moment. As we finished our conversation, I felt that the angels were rejoicing in heaven. Then I dismissed that feeling. We both moved toward each other, uncontrollably pulled, and we kissed, and that was when I knew. In my vision, I saw us standing in the middle of heaven surrounded by white clouds. I saw a marriage, and this is when he and I transferred the breath of life into one another. The breath of life went on for one minute, and I felt the air leaving my body, then going to him, and returning to me. I forcefully pulled away. I didn't tell him what I saw or felt. He stared at me, and I said, "Okay, we'll talk later," and I left.

When I got in my car, I saw a text from him. "Wow, what was that feeling?" he said. I was glad I was not facing this fearful yet beautiful moment alone. I went home and pondered. We were both in a messed-up situation. We were both experiencing something greater than ourselves.

The meetings went on every once in a while, where we would talk. After a year had passed, I wondered where the time went. We had not even had sex yet. This one guy who I liked and had something special with did not sleep with me? I became confused, because I thought sex was connected to love. Our meet-ups were still about confessing our sins. Then I realized my time with him and the kiss alone were great. It was the highest feeling I had ever felt.

Then, the time came. After one year and a couple of months, we headed to a hotel room. I was nervous as a virgin. I walked into the room and took a shower. I wanted to stay in the bathroom for hours and not go near him. I didn't know if I didn't deserve the feeling or if I was fearful of it. I walked out of the bathroom with a white towel wrapped around me. There he was lying on the bed. He looked confused, excited, and nervous. I dropped the towel and got on top of him. After a couple of strokes, we both stopped and realized we couldn't move forward.

I don't even recall what happened. I just remember I was lying in the bed ready to go to sleep, and I looked over to my side. He was sleeping. It was three in the morning, and I knew he had to be home because he was still married. I fell asleep until I heard him wake up. He looked at his phone. "Shit," he said. He placed his hand over his head. I knew he had some explaining to do to his wife. For the first time, I felt his heart hurting through my own heart. I lay there and felt the feeling of silence as I watched him walk out the door.

CHAPTER

13

Starting a New Journey

THE SUMMER OF 2011 was almost over, and the kids were starting school back up again. It had been one year without me working and doing my inner work. God knows when to send us help, and I was not mentally prepared to take my kids to school. My mom has been my spiritual strength, and I thank God for her love and support. I remember asking the Lord for a job experience again. Deep in my heart, I always knew I had a higher calling and purpose that would bring me great depression and happiness in return. After weeks of ignoring a Pennysaver that came in the mail for job posting, the third time caused my heart to palpitate. I filled out an application, and they called me the next day.

During the interview, she stated the starting pay was nine dollars an hour. I was wondering if it was a sick joke! It wasn't, and it was serving adults with intellectual disabilities. I didn't know what the Lord was up to. Nor did I know how I was going to make it, earning less than I had been making at the hospital. I knew I was starting a new journey.

I proceeded with the unknown, accepting the offer. I studied metaphysical science. During my studies, I obtained a metaphysical minister's certificate and metaphysical practitioner's diploma. I had transferred my kids' to another school. During tax season refund was a way to buy my car and start moving my life forward. It had been months since I had heard from the teacher, and I did not bother to contact him either. I didn't want to figure out what was going on between us that was beyond my knowledge and experience. We both had a lot going on. He was still married, and I was going through a separation period and waiting for divorce. We did not need that type of confusion during that period of our lives. I wanted him to be happy and work out whatever he had to do. However, he still came into my thoughts often.

There was a coworker of mine who supported me in many ways. I didn't know if it was a curse or blessing, but I got to see the light and dark reflection from this soul connection. She was the house manager. As she started her orientation session with me, she explained, "If you do not like wiping butts, then this is not the job for you. We clean, take individuals on outings, and wipe butts, all day long!"

I thought, *It's my time to exit out the front door!* Then I thought about the parable when Jesus said, "The Student is not above the teacher, but everyone who is fully trained will be like their teacher" (Luke 6:40). I kindly said to her, "I am aware of the services I will be providing to the clients. My background experience is in the hospital, and I am currently a college student."

Her perception of me changed, and she said, "Why are you here?"

I know that I am in full training from my master, the Almighty himself. I could not expect to see the fruit of my labor without experiencing it all. I know what it feels like to be sad, angry, mad, happy, close to death, and in poverty. At the time of my encounter with her, I was at the lowest poverty point of my life. I was in an awakened stage of learning about myself. I had gone almost one full year without working or shopping. As she guided me upstairs, I was checking out my hair. It had been some time since I had it done. We finally finished up the orientation, and I spoke to God within me to make sure this was where I wanted to be at the moment. I started a conversation with her about the Lord, and she went on telling me about her divinity studies.

Then I shared my experiences with visions and miracles that had happened to me. She said, "That is practicing witchcraft?"

"No, I do not practice witchcraft. These things happen to me, and it was an experience."

She went back and forth and said, "God said that is demonic!"

Then I paused. "Let's just say a form of magic has been taking place my whole life, without me being consciously aware of it."

She looked at me and said, "You have the gift. That is a blessing. You are the blessed one!"

It was the second time in my life people used that term to describe me. I said, "I am sure we all have the gift but do not use it."

I was sitting on the sofa with one of the individuals. He had dementia. He was the cutest old man I had ever seen. He was in his fifties and loved to give hugs and kisses. The front doorbell rang. The individual said, "Who is it?" He laughed. His laughter tickled me. I opened the front door, and no one was standing there.

My coworker said, "Is the door ringing again without no one

there? Well, my dear, you are in the right house. Many spirits we do not see visit the individuals." I looked at her and spoke to the Lord in my head because I remembered the encounter with my ex-boyfriend's spirit. I was not going down that road of craziness again.

Later that night, the door rang again. It was around ten o'clock. I opened it, and an old lady stormed passed me and went downstairs. I said to myself, *Rude bitch.* I went back upstairs. "Who was that?" my coworker asked.

"I guess it's the other coverage release to work?"

"What release?" she said. "I'm off the clock. You will be working the nightshift, 11:00 p.m. to 7:00 a.m. alone."

"Well, who was that lady I let in the door?" I said.

"Oh Lord, you let someone in?"

"Yes. She was rude when I said hi."

"There is no one supposed to be here, Cindy!" We both ran to the kitchen and grabbed big butcher knives and proceeded to walk downstairs in the basement.

"You go first since you're the one that let her in," she said.

I thought, *Huh!* Then I took a deep breath and walked downstairs. I started to remember the lady's face in my mind, and she was a little transparent. We opened all doors, pulled back the bathroom curtain, and checked everywhere. She said, "No one's here." Then I stood in the middle of the floor. My face was red. I couldn't breathe. She said, "What is wrong with you?"

"The lady that walked in was a ghost/spirit," I said.

She stared at me. "Did you see her?"

"Yes."

I didn't tell her about my encounter with a spirit before. I wasn't scared that I saw it again. I was afraid now because I had to be in the house alone with someone I called a bad name.

I was working on my college papers while a client was getting in the bed. I saw my coworker getting ready to leave out the door. She had on some black tights and a fitted black blouse. She stood about five nine and weighed 220 pounds. Her glamorous heels matched her glamorous red, shiny lipstick. I hadn't been out for so long; I didn't even know where to start with shopping and clothing styles.

So, I said to her, "You look very nice. Where are you heading to?"

"I am going to a Baltimore nightclub to dance. I love to dance," she said.

"Aw, that's nice. Me too." "It's been so long since I been out," I said.

"Why don't you come along next time?"

"I don't know. I have nothing nice to wear." I chuckled. "Look at my hair."

"That is an easy fix," she said. I finished up my school papers after she left, and I was glad the spirit did not come for me that night.

Two weeks later, to my surprise, I had bought black high heels. They had a small bow on them and a strap that went around my thin ankles. I had on fitted jeans and a light blue see-through blouse. My hair had extra pieces in it—a weave with the color of mocha and tan highlights that matched the color of my skin. My skin tone was light mocha. The only makeup I chose to use was light gray eyeshadow, mascara, and shiny lip gloss. You know what that means. Time to manifest my dream man! Party time.

CHAPTER

14

Protection

I DIDN'T FULLY UNDERSTAND why, after all these years, I was still looking for the one. The one who would be my fairy tale. I also did some strange things before walking into nightclubs. I would think, *Okay, Lord, let's do this! I am going to make this a night to remember!* I went inside a lounge and sat down at the bar. That place was jumping on a Friday night. The DJ was on point with mixing the music. To the left was my delight! "Eres tan sexy," I said to a Puerto Rican. He was the bouncer that night. He stood posted up against the wall with his black uniform on and his gun. He looked sexy but weary.

I decided to dance with him that night. Everyone was wondering why the bouncer was off duty to dance with me. I went back to the bar where I met my cock blocker. He was the one who distracted me from the bouncer. "Can I buy you a drink?" he said.

"Well, do you honestly think your drink will smooth me over?"

I thought, *Did I stumble over my words?* Everything was coming out of my mouth in truth.

I said, "Excuse me one second" as I placed one finger up. I went back to talk to the bouncer. "Hi, handsome fella!"

My coworker pulled me to the side. "Are you aware what you are doing?"

"Yes, I am trying to choose between A and C. Did she say why C and not B? He's about to C his way home." I chuckled.

"Oh Lord, you're drunk," she said.

"I am fully aware of my situation. I am just having fun."

"Well, it does not look like your little Romeo and hold on over there is having fun with you."

"Okay," I said.

I jumped up toward the bouncer, and he embraced me in his arms, but then came the cock blocker. He yelled, "Get down from there!"

The bouncer said, "Is that your boyfriend?"

"No, I don't know him. His name is the blocker!"

"Hey, woman, that is not my name," he said.

"He is acting like your boyfriend tonight," my coworker said.

"I am out of here," my coworker said. "I will be outside until you figure your mess out." I said goodbye to the bouncer. He told me he was going to see a priest in another country and did not know when he would be returning. He was going to be clearing karma from his life. I could not believe I heard that at the lounge.

I went outside to skip along the side as I danced toward the car to meet my coworker. That was where the guy who already claimed me (cock blocker) stood at her truck. He looked pissed! "Hello," I said.

"Get in the car," he said. He pointed his gun toward my back.

"Hey, put your little toy away," I said.

"Oh Lord, he has a gun!" my coworker yelled.

"Calm down. I am here to protect her," he said. "Get in, and I will follow you to your safety," he said.

"I don't know about this, Cindy," she said.

"Well, let's just see," I replied.

CHAPTER

15

Returning Home

IN WAS 2012. MY ex-husband and I had some agreements and an arrangement for the kids. He was taking the older son, who was now going to the first grade. He had full custody of the oldest because he did not want to pay child support. Of course, he did not stick to the agreement. I had my youngest son, who was going to prekindergarten, but it was a separate school from where my oldest son was. I ended up getting a one-bedroom. My oldest daughter was with her grandma, and my youngest daughter lived with her aunt. The one-bedroom apartment was comfortable for my son and me.

However, during my move back to the county, I saw a text that said, "Hi!" It was the teacher. I didn't understand how he knew I was returning because I didn't tell anyone at the time. I was dating the guy from the club and had finally gotten a divorce. The last person I needed showing up was him! I did not answer the text at that time, but I later found out he was going to be at the school that my youngest son who was attending pre-K would be at. I was stuck and could not hide.

School was starting back up in three weeks, and the teacher had to transfer the kids' toys from one location to another. He told me he would be there if I was not busy that week. I agreed and showed up.

As I was walking up the stairs to the school, I felt I should turn around. I did not want to be pulled into that magnetic attraction and deal with the emotional relationship I was having with the guy from the club. I peeked inside the door of the classroom where he stood moving the toys around. I stood there thinking, *I wanted that life with him. He was the one I wanted to share babies and a lifelong journey with.* I stood at the door for a few minutes before walking in.

"Hello, and how have you been?" he said.

"I am fine." I wanted to say, "Where in the hell did you go after all these years?" I realized I couldn't ask him the question without asking myself the question because I was running too. I sat down to wipe off the kitchen toy set in the play area. I saw myself playing with the toys as a little girl, and he was playing house with me. I saw it all in a vision.

He came to break my fantasy and said as he smiled, "We are going to be married in five years."

I looked up and wondered if was he reading my thoughts—and why five years?

"I have a lot to clean up in my life. When I finish, I am going to have you," he said. I nodded. What he did not know is I had gotten myself into another situation. I was having men problems.

Then I thought back to when he confessed his sins to me. He had many women, more than he could count. I saw that also in myself, with men. The more I talked to him, I realized it was a lot of my mess I had to fix. I did not want to face what was in my soul. There were no more occasional meetups after that. It was only hi and hello in the form of a text message. I felt like I wanted to prepare for him in secret. I thought, *How will I do that?*

The guy from the club I was dating was a security guard, and he became my partner. I saw a lot of potential in him. I didn't understand why he sold himself short with his career life, dreams, and goals. We lived together for two years. Around this time, the teacher informed me he was separated. In my heart, I knew he needed to heal. Me showing up around this time was not best for his healing. I prayed he would find himself. A security guard is a family man. He did not have kids. He had gray hair already at the age of thirty. His lifelong dream was to be a police officer, and I watched him drink himself toward death.

I want to beat him because I felt my emotions when I was with him. He was the first guy who took me to his family church. I was feeling connected to him, and it made me want to beat him even more! He surrounded me with the family lifestyle, and our dinner dates were always Thursday nights, and this went on even after living together.

One night in a dream, I saw myself walking around in the room where I was lying down to sleep. It looked like my exact bedroom, and I would have thought it was not a dream if it hadn't been for a few things out of place. There he was lying on the bed in the same spot before I fell asleep. I heard a woman under the bed crying. I looked under, and there she was balled up under the bed on my side. I jumped out of my dream. I decide to do some investigation. I reached for my partner's Google password and his phone. To my surprise, there were plenty of women he misled in writing and texts, making a promise to meet them, though he never did. I didn't know if I should beat him in his sleep or wait for him to wake up. I took my hand and slapped it across his head.

He stood up as if he had seen a ghost. "Why are you misleading women!" He looked at me and never said he didn't. I grabbed him, but he blocked me. We rolled around on the floor, tumbling to fight, but why was I fighting him? He didn't see these women. I wanted to destroy him because he was digging too deep into my emotions. I grabbed his laptop and stomped on it with my wedge heel. He said, "That does not hurt me."

Our days and nights went on calmly, and we went back to family time—until another night when I had a dream he was at work, and his boss said, "I am sorry, but we have to terminate you." He walked away sad. I woke up that morning. This time, he woke up before me.

I stared at him and did not know how I was going to break the news to him. He said, "What, you're having more of your dreams?" He laughed.

"Well, you think it's funny? Let me reveal to you the truth. Your boss is going to fire you!" Two weeks later, he got fired for the wrongfully misleading woman.

All my items went flying toward his head, and he used everything he learned in defense training to block it and me. I learned from him that I had my dreams to fulfill. I had to leave that relationship and continue to find myself.

I moved back to the county and allowed him to stay in my old apartment until the lease was up. I wanted to stay away from men and continue to work on myself. From 2014 to 2015, I spend much time alone. I went back to working out and finished up my college degree.

I was just trying to find my happy place in life. In 2015, I picked up another job at a medical center, and in 2017, I left. I spent most of my time in nature and by the water. I was still employed working with adults with intellectual disability, on call.

CHAPTER

16

Know Thyself

I WAS LOVING BEING single and alone. It felt refreshing. I ran every morning for forty minutes. I went to a Whole Foods store. I looked at how beautiful the fruits and cuts of meats were, and I enjoyed the beauty of it. I had cleared out a lot of past life experiences. I thought the clearing was over.

I proceeded to the checkout line when I saw a guy who looked about twenty-three years old, five eight and about 120 pounds. He was the smallest guy I had ever seen. He had on skinny jeans. He wore a nose ring and was brown skinned, with light blond tips on his brown, twisted hair. He was a different kind of African American. He had on Adidas shoes, and later I found out that he hated Nike boots and the traditional black man clothing. He was in love with Egyptian clothing. I stood in the line figuring out how I was going to approach him while he was working. It was my turn, and he began to ring me up. He had a bit of nervousness in his voice as he said, "Hello."

I said, "What's good?" I brought myself down to his language and tone to get the vibe with him. He smiled. I said, "You seem like a nice guy. I love your shirt. Are you into Buddha teaching?"

"Yes, I am a spiritual person," he said. "I am trying to figure it all out. I am more into Egypt and our ancestors." I did not know much about Egypt. However, I was into Buddha's teachings at the time because they seemed to explain my spiritual journey. I liked studying charkas, and I was experiencing a kundalini awakening. It is a feminine evolutionary force of infinite wisdom that lives within all of us.

"I could be your mentor/teacher," I said.

He smiled and said, "Sure!"

I put his number into my phone and left the store. As I walked outside, I thought, *What are you doing? You know you are not going to be his mentor. When are you going to give up control over these men?* Then I heard another voice inside say, "Never!"

I met up with him a week later. He did not drive, and he lived with his mom. He got in my car and asked, "Why me? Should you be married or something?"

"I'm good," I said.

I started to listen to myself and noticed my language changed toward him. Then I said, "You are very wise for a young man." We went on to talk about his Egyptian culture and how the land was taken. I saw darkness in his soul.

"They took the land; they stole the damn land from our ancestors!" He was angry.

We went to the park. We walked around, and there was this one black crow. The black crow held his eyes toward me. Then the guy stood in front of me and stared at the same black crow that stared at me. The crow turned around with his back facing the guy. "Wow," I said. "Did he turn away from you?"

He said, "Fuck that crow."

I thought, *Who would say that to an animal?* My heart started to beat fast. He held me in his arms, and I pulled away. "I cannot be here to clear your darkness."

"What darkness?" he said.

I went on to let him hug me and thought I should forget about it for the moment. I started to tell my story about how men were mistreating me. I did not trust them, and in that moment, I knew it was a deep-rooted issue that was coming up from childhood. I felt my anger rising, back from being in the apartment when I was young!

The guy listened as he moved in to show me love, but I blocked it. He said, "You are not a victim. Let it go! You cannot expect to move forward. I am not going to sit here so you can hurt me," he argued. We both were angry. The darkness that was in him was still in me. I didn't tell him at the time. I should have left the connection altogether. I knew I hated men. All my relationships with men were about me having full control. It was always my place, and all the bills were in my name. When I was ready to leave the relationships, I did. I never let anyone close to my heart. The one that seemed to be already in my heart was the one I avoided. The teacher.

The guy saw straight through me. I wanted to distract him from knowing I was abusing men (unconsciously). At the time, I was not aware of it. So, I slept with the guy. For me, it was only sex. He came close to hugging and embracing me again, but I moved to the other side of the bed. I recalled that this was my pattern with men. He stood up and grabbed his clothes.

He pointed his finger at my forehead, and my head started to move back and forth as he jammed his finger into it. He said, "You are not going to shit on me and leave me like you did the rest of them!" Then he did the same thing toward my heart and said, "Open this shit up!"

He was right. I was not a victim, and it was not my father's fault, or my ex-husband's or boyfriend's. It was my darkness, and I needed to fix myself. I was abusing men and angry with them. The one person who I said I would not be like, I was just like. The vibration of hate and strong emotion had drawn my dad's spirit within me. I sat in the middle of my bed, becoming more aware of myself. The guy said, "Look at you. You are a witch!"

"What are you saying?" I said.

"Look at your hands in the Buddha position. Your thumb and index finger touching. Legs crossed over!" I looked down at myself, and for the first time, I noticed I was in the oneness position. It was my way of being in control and keeping everyone out of my inside world. "No wonder you're so happy. Hurting everyone around you?" he said.

The truth was I was not always happy, and I had not known I was sitting in the Buddha position. It was something that happened naturally for me. I received the message that I was hurting people. I forgave myself and everyone. He accepted it and walked away! When I tried to reach out to him, he blocked me. I do not blame him.

Just when I became aware of myself and thought it was over, I entered a female strip club. The Chinese owner smiled at me when I walked in and let me in free of charge. I said to myself, *Don't even think about it. I am not here to be a stripper.* Why was I there? I sat at the bar drinking a Long Island. My coworker was with me. "I don't know about this, but if you want to, let's go," she had said.

She didn't know about my sexual encounter with a woman. I did not learn from the experience. Did I have to repeat it? I didn't see any females I liked in there, and it was good for me. I sat having a conversation with my coworker and men at the bar. When I turned around, I saw this skinny stripper who approached me with a dance. "Oh Lord, get her away," my coworker said. "We're not gay or bisexual, so bye!"

She was light brown, about twenty-five, weighed about 115 pounds, and stood about five eight. She had little breasts, and they seemed to be sagging. I could tell she had at least one child. Her butt was even small. My coworker threw her Long Island liquor on the girl. The guards were about to put her out until they were shocked by my actions.

As the Long Island was running down her breasts, I went toward her and put my tongue toward the part that was dripping down. "What in the world? Is there something you wanted to tell me?" my coworker criticized. "You are full of surprises, lady!" When I looked up, I saw my ex-boyfriend security guy entering the strip club. He saw me and went back out. I ran after him.

"What are you doing here?" I said.

"Wait, what are *you* doing here?" he responded. A lightbulb went off in my head. I realized why I beat him, for misleading women. I was beating myself up as well and not fulfilling my purpose. I didn't answer his question and went back inside the strip club.

I met back up with my coworker, who was still asking me to explain myself. Then on the side, the stripper bought me a drink. I went back into a state of depression but could not feel it at the time because I was numb from drinking. I took the drink the stripper offered me, got her number, and headed out.

I got in the car. I drove my coworker and myself back to the county where we lived. It was a forty-five-minute drive, and to this day, I cannot understand how I ended up in my bed. I do not recall driving at all. At that time, I started to sense a higher calling on my life, and I was ignoring it and playing around on earth.

In the morning, I explained the female situation to my coworker. There had been two encounters in my life, and I had sex with both of them.

That same day, around noon, I met the stripper at the bar. I walked in the door and sat down. I noticed she had a white older man sitting next to her. He was talking about selling his Mercedes Benz. I could see straight through the conversation. The car was going be free for one of us if we engaged in some freaky stuff. I was not down for that kind of pay. Then I thought, *Why not? I am doing it for free anyway.* I learned it was not something I had to experience. I gave the girl a look that I was not down for it. She cut the conversation short with him and left with me.

I found myself in her apartment, drinking on her sofa. I had sex with her. I put on my clothes, proceeded to leave, and told her I was going to call her. I knew I was not. She asked for forty dollars to pay her electric bill. I placed the money on the table and left. I felt like I was going to get sick. I went in my car. *Did I pay a stripper for sex?* I went home and never again slept with another woman. Not only did my life change, but her life changed too. She stopped stripping and currently works at a bank.

CHAPTER

17

Synchronicity

I WAS AT A point in my life where I should have left men alone, once again. I was at my house, sitting on the edge of my bed. It was the most pain I had felt in years—the pain from the security guard. Pulling away from that connection was like pulling up roots from a tree. The pain from the teacher was the separation. I decided not to move along in my life until I figured out those two energies. I got dressed and went to Quiet Waters Park. It was where I went to find peace.

I would jog for an hour, and at the end of the path was this beautiful water that connected to the bay. It was where I met the Lord first thing in the morning. While jogging, at the end of the path, I would imagine the Lord inside the bay, talking through energy as the water moved. I heard the water say, "This is the way life goes. Right along the beautiful path." I knew at that point nothing in life was an accident; it was all an experience. It was about learning and growing.

One night, I was getting back from my mom's house after dropping the kids off to spend the night. It was my time alone. When I walked in my front door, I felt the air. It was a weird feeling, as if other souls in my house were walking around. It was many souls. It was my first time experiencing it, so I couldn't decipher the meaning. I headed toward the bathroom. As I sat on the toilet, I felt it again. Have you ever closed your eyes when lying down and felt people walking into your room or past you? That was what I felt. However, I didn't see anybody. I flushed the toilet and went to my room. Down toward my foot, I saw my bank statement on the floor. Then I looked around, wondering why it was on the floor when it should have been in the closet on top of my safe box. My safe box used to have spare money of $2,000, but I had decided to move it out last week and use it for my important documents. I looked up on the shelf in my closet, and the safe box was gone!

I headed for the kitchen, where the wind got even stronger. The kitchen had a back door. That was where I stood in silence. I did not move at first. My eyes examined the broken back door. I took my finger and traced it down the door lock where it was hanging down on the floor; the door could not close. It was wide open, allowing air to pass through. I looked around in the kitchen for other clues; I found nothing. I went back to my room and saw all my boy's new clothes and shoes that I had purchased that day on the bed. They still had tags on them, and the shoe bags were worth more than $200. I was wondering why the thief did not take it.

As I proceeded to walk upstairs, I stopped. *Wait. What am I doing? Why didn't I call the police?* At that moment, I knew I was walking in the boldness of the spirit. However, I became aware of my flesh, and I started to get scared. I stood in the middle of my living room and heard my dog bark. It was a Maltese chihuahua, and her fur was white with a little brown in it. Her name was Mercedes. I named her that because, in my vision, I saw myself driving one. I opened the basement door and pulled her into my arms.

I took my cell phone out of my back pocket and phoned the police. He instructed me to wait outside. I saw two security guards sitting in their car, and I shook my head. As the police pulled up to my unit, the security guards jumped out of the car and raced over. I gave my report to one police officer as the other one went inside to check the home. The security guard started talking to me as the officer was documenting. I said, "Wait a minute. You guys were sitting outside the whole time and saw nothing? When was the last time you patrolled on foot?" They kept quiet, and the police officer stared at me as I questioned the guards. "Excuse me one second while I speak with the officer," I said.

I wrote a report on the security guards sitting in the car while a burglary was taking place and put it in the property manager's box outside the rental office door. I expected to hear from them in the morning. The officer came out and said, "Do you have somewhere to stay for the night? You should not stay here with the door broken until it gets fixed."

One place I was not going was to my parents' house again. I still had a key to my old apartment where my ex-boyfriend was staying. I phoned him to let him know I was coming. When I entered, he was getting ready to leave to go to the club. I couldn't be mad because that was where I met him, and we were not together. I sat on the living room floor with my dog. My ex looked at me and said, "Well, did you call the police?" I sat staring at him without saying a word and thought, *Such a dummy.* I lay on the floor and rested my eyes.

All I wanted was protection because my heart was aching. I balled myself into a knot on the floor, with my arms wrapped around me as he walked out the front door.

Tears were forming in my eyes. I could not stop them. I stared at the floor and recalled my life events. Why was I still facing challenges? I thought, *The truth shall pass. If no one is there, I am going to be here for myself.* My tears flowed even faster as I drifted off to sleep.

I got up the next morning and did not even say goodbye to him. It was around three in the morning when he came home drunk. I walked out the front door. I knew in my soul that any relationship for us was over for good, and there was no turning back. I called the rental office, and I had to pay for them to fix my door. My brother gave me information about an alarm system. I lay in my bed trying to figure out, *Who did it?* I played the feeling and vision in my head over and over. A part of me wanted them to come back so I could beat them down. Then I realized I should forgive them and let it go.

I was at work when I thought, *About a day ago, someone broke into my house.* I received a call from one of the program managers, letting me know that I should report to the C4 building instead of my regular unit. I was not in the mood for change, but I went anyway. As I walked in the door, I noticed I was working with a guy who was the house manager at the time. He was only twenty-three years old.

I spoke to the other worker who I would be replacing and got some information on the individual I would be providing care for. As the guy was going to the front door, I glared at him. He seemed arrogant. Everyone left, and it was the house manager, the individuals, and me there. I sat on the sofa away from him. It had been some time since I had been away from men, and I wanted to continue to do that. Then I remembered that weeks ago I had placed a request into the Lord that I wanted to experience a peaceful guy.

He broke the silence and asked, "Are you watching TV?"

"I do not watch TV as much. I do a lot of reading."

"May I ask what you read?" he asked. We got into a conversation about spiritual connections.

I looked at my watch and saw the time; soon I would be heading to a bar with a coworker to have a few drinks. So, I ended the conversation with him. I told him where I would be that night if he wanted to go. He gave me his number. I made sure he had mine too. I did not want to make the first contact. I left at the end of my shift.

As I met my coworker at the bar, I told her I might be having a guest. "You are going to do that again? I thought you were going to take a long break from it," she said.

"I have been on a long break. Besides, I don't know if he will come or not. So let's just go in and have fun!"

She ordered and paid for me to have a blue motorcycle drink. It tasted good yet strong and different. I decided to keep drinking. I noticed my eyes getting tired. I needed rest. We had a few more drinks before heading out.

We were standing outside. There were a couple of guys starting to talk to us, and I do not recall what they said because I was not interested in them, and their faces were a blur to me. I thought, *Did someone put something in my drink?* I proceeded to go to my car while she got in her own at the end of the street. This nice-looking white guy followed me and started asking for my number. I told him I was not in the mood to talk. I got in my car. I wanted to rest my head but also wanted to drive straight home. Then I realized I had to be at work at seven in the morning, and it was already two.

As I was driving, I saw the green light in multiple directions and knew something was wrong with me. I passed out while driving, which had never happened to me before. I jumped up and noticed I was driving in the wrong direction on the street.

My heart started to race, and the only way back over was to move through the fork in the middle of the road. I did not realize it was going to mess up my whole car. It damaged the side of the tire, leaving it unable to change or bear the condition of continuing driving. I prayed to God that the police would not give me a DUI and send me to jail. I managed to drive it off to the side and called a coworker to pick me up.

He took the risk of leaving the job and took us back to the place where we both worked. Not the C4 building. As I looked up, I remembered how handsome he was. He had caramel skin, light brown eyes, and a smile that melted me. "Dang, you drunk," he said. He wrapped his arms around me and said, "You good?" To my surprise, being in his loving arms led to sexual energy. After it was complete, I rolled over on the sofa and went to sleep. He tried to roll over with me, but I told him there was no room for two.

Three days later, he came to the table where I was sitting at work. He grabbed my phone and ran downstairs. "Bring my phone back!" I yelled. The clients were staring at me, and I became emotional. He came back upstairs and threw my phone at me. I laughed and said, "What is your problem?" He lifted me up in the air and slammed me back down, then dragged me to the bottom of the steps. "Would you stop?" I said. "We're working, you know."

"You out here breaking men's hearts?"

"No, I am not. They hurt me!"

"Who hurt you? From the looks of your text messages in your phone, you hurt all of them. You a female player?"

I wrapped my arms around me to defend myself. I rocked back and forth in the dining room chair and thought, *Who hurt me?* Tears formed in my eyes.

I phoned my coworker the next day. "We need to talk. Could we meet for drinks?" I asked.

"Sure! See you at seven," she replied.

We both got there and sat outside at a table. She looked at me. "What's wrong?"

"I am having men problems."

"The only problem you're having is with yourself." She chuckled. Then I looked up and stared at the waiter who was bringing our drinks to the table. I shook my head because it was not the time for him to show up.

"Go on. I'm listening. What kind of problems are you having?"

"Be quiet for now; we have a guest approaching the table," I said.

"Girl, please. He's just the bartender bringing our drinks."

"Not just any bartender. You tell him I'm shy. I want to talk to him," I said.

"What? I thought you came here to talk," she complained.

"I did, but this is important. He's on his way. So tell him!"

He approached the table. He had a Mohawk fade, and it was full of nice loose curls. "Well, my friend wants your number," she said. "She's shy."

"She's cute," he replied.

I put on the shy, blushing face, looked up, and said, "Hi!"

He said, "I'm working, but I get off at eleven, and we will have plenty of time to talk." He slid his number over to me. He left to serve the rest of the tables.

"So, what's up, girl?" she said.

"I did something horrible. I slept with brown-eyes at the job."

She coughed on her drink. "You did what? You know you just opened up a can of worms, right? You just met the guy from the C-4 building." She shook her head.

"Oh well, that's out of my system. Let's drink!" I declared.

"You sure you're not a man?" she said.

That night, I met the guy from the bar. We sat on his sofa at his mom's house. He was twenty-seven years old. I thought, *Why doesn't he have his own place?*

He looked at me and said, "I am a Mason."

"What is that?" I asked. "Illuminati?" I had heard bad stories about it, and he was nowhere near the description of the people I had heard described. We sat on the sofa watching TV.

"I feel something," he observed.

"You do?" I said.

"Yes, someone is walking up to the door and about to knock."

One, two, three, and there was the knock. I turned to him and knew he had the same sensitive feeling I have toward energy, but what was the Illuminati?

"Fear not, your part in the Universal Design. You are safe, and help is on the way! Do not be afraid of the stricken poverty planet. Design your path for the human species for prosperity. It is not enough land, wealth or food, and war is all a lie! The universe is full of abundance. Fear not for the birthing pain but prepare for the light that is growing within you. I am the Illuminati." (The first testament of Illuminati, n.d)

The guy came to my house to visit. I did not have a TV in my room because I did not watch it. If it did not promote my spiritual growth, there was no need to feed my subconscious mind. We both looked at each other and got down to business. After sex, he brushed me off as I went near him. He did not have to say it verbally; I received the message. He sensed many souls over my body. It was time for me to be careful of the body temple. It affected my energy. Our soul tie was over!

While I was stuck in the middle of the road and drunk, I vowed that if God got me out of that situation, I would never drink again. I should never have vowed a promise to the Lord. I learned my lesson. On another occasion, I had another drink, and I woke up in a hospital bed with two IVs running in my arm. I was shaking as if I was going thorough withdrawal.

The more I meditated, the more I noticed the alcohol becoming toxic inside me. The nurse ran over to my room as the machine was going off. I started to sweat, and she asked me, "Have you been taking drugs?"

"No." My migraine was not under control. I started vomiting and had a panic attack.

I spoke to the Lord after my deliverance from the emergency department. I was sorry for making promises. However, since that experience, I no longer drink alcohol. Until this day, I have no desire to drink liquor. I have occasional red wine Sangria.

It was nine in the morning when I saw a text on my phone:

"Good morning, beautiful," with a heart behind it. It was the guy from the C4 building at work. I stared at the phone and wondered if I was going to go through with talking or not. I didn't have to see his face again because that was not my regular work building. Instead of listening to my thoughts, I texted back, "Good morning!"

We got together to have dinner at a restaurant. Our conversation was short, and it seemed to be quiet at the table while we both sat and ate. When returning to the car, we both noticed the clock read 11:11. We looked at each other and stared. "I have seen that number every day lately," he said. I thought, *It is strange that I am seeing it with him. It pricks at my heart because I feel a meaning behind it.* I looked further into the meaning behind the number, and it stated: awakening, pay attention to your thoughts, and remember who you are.

I was starting to wonder if he was my life partner because we were experiencing synchronicity. As he and I continued to spend more time together, he never went home. He had his townhouse, but he always stayed the night at my house. We both agreed to walk a path to stay away from negative thinking, friends, and the club. During my time spend with him, I noticed the other guy with the light brown eyes kept calling me. He knew him too, because we all worked together. "Did you have sex with him?" he asked.

"No!" I wanted to tell him the truth, but it wasn't the time. Besides, did he reveal his secrets to me yet? Light-eyes was the cutest, and all the females wanted him.

Walking up to the guy's townhouse, I saw a car next door that looked like that of light-brown-eyes. "Is that his car?" I said.

"You mean the one that keeps calling your phone? His baby mother and he live there together. Why you are rushing in the house?

I thought you did not have sex with him. Looks like your heart is beating fast to me," he said.

"No, I told you I didn't!" I cut the soul tie off with brown-eyes. I knew why he came. He came to reveal the cause of my pain.

Nine months later, the guy from the C4 building and I leased an apartment together. After two years, we were still in a relationship, and I noticed I could not fit in my jeans. I got on the scale, and my weight had gone from 140 pounds to 190. That was the biggest I had ever been. Even when I was carrying a child, I never reached that weight.

It was time for me to step back and live in my truth. What was I doing wrong? I had cut off all my friends. I had stopped talking to the security guard and my coworker and did not contact the teacher. I could not remember the last time I had jogged or was in nature, which I loved so much. I looked down and saw myself as a fat mushroom. Everyone else saw me as thick, and I just filled out my figure. We had arguments because he went on many trips with his best friend, and it had been two years, and I had not seen any of my friends. I was suffocating myself unconsciously.

I stopped working at the medical center because that was part of my stress. I was not using my gifts and talents there. After five months, I lost ten pounds, but blocked energy was still inside of me.

I started walking in nature again. I knew I had a lot of work to do. I needed to gain my strength and power back. I had given him my power because we both had seen the synchronicity, and I believed we were on a life-partner journey together. After two years and some months in a relationship with him, I started to reach out to all my friends whom I had ignored over the years, hoping they would forgive me.

The first person I contacted was my coworker. We spoke, and she said, "I knew it was unlike you." I went to a bar with her that night and invited him to join us. She looked at me, and I knew what that look meant. "What happened to you?" she said. "You're not dancing? You have lost yourself in him," she whispered.

I realized I was helping him get his dreams and goals off the ground and noticed I did not seek help for myself. I had no one to talk to about my spiritual journey, so I stopped. He was only reflecting to me what I had taught him. I thought we were on the same path. I should have interpreted the message as I was growing because I didn't attract someone who caused me pain emotionally or physically. He was peace because I was peace. However, he should never have become my peace. I am the peace that I seek!

I was glad I encouraged him to get his driver's license, which allowed him to get a second job driving. He also started his graphic design business. I stepped back to look at my life, and it was time for me to step into my purpose. I looked over at my phone and noticed the teacher had requested me as a friend on Facebook. We did not talk for years, but we could see how the other was doing on social media. Then I noticed none of my other male friends were connected to me on social media, only him. It made me became aware of this journey. I looked at my current partner's social media and noticed there was just one picture of us; it was a picture he designed. On my page were over twenty of the time we spent together.

It was time for me to cut the ties. Before I did, I wanted to play a game. Christmas was the day I said to him, "Let's play a game." He was excited to do so, and he smiled. The game was called, "Do I know you?"

I grabbed a piece of paper and gave him a sheet as well. I

explained, "You will tell me all my friends, including males and females, that I shared with you. You will also tell me the place I want to travel to and where I love to spend my time."

He smiled. "To start, your best friend is China (who I did not mention in this book), India (who I did not speak about), your coworker (my party soul), security guard, and the teacher," he said.

"Great, you covered all the basics." He smiled. "Where would I like to go?"

"You want to travel to Paris," he said.

"Finally, one more question. Where do I love to spend my time?"

"In nature and by the water."

"Wonderful! So I shared with you my deepest desires and the souls that were important to me. Great job," I said.

"Okay, my turn. Who is my best friend?"

I said, "That's easy: Mathew. That's the one you told me you traveled with to Vegas while we were together. Next?"

He stared at me and stopped. I looked at him. He could not go on because he had kept his life a secret from me.

The game became a nightmare for him. I said, "Do you understand what I was trying to get you to see? I am not trying to hurt you. I want you to see where I immersed myself in you. I know nothing about you. I do not know your desires. What do you love? I told you my darkest secret of sleeping with a woman. You just sat and listened." I stood up from the sofa. I saw myself laying it down at the cross. I forgave him and myself.

When I came back in full union with myself, I saw a message in my inbox from the teacher that said, "Hi." The hi and hello went back and forth for six months.

Finally, I decided to say I could meet him. He did not respond.

Then he said that he could visit me, but I did not reply. I knew for sure I was not ready, and I had a lot of cleaning up to do once again. I was at work around noon on a Saturday when I received a message from the teacher. I decided I should stop running. So, we met at the park.

I stood away from his car, peeking because I felt myself getting nervous. I felt a tingling in my body that was bringing me back to a higher vibration. The car stood between us. I was hoping he would stay on that side, and not come near, and I could hear my soul calling for the divine. We both sat in the vehicle. We spoke for two hours. Then I remembered I was on the clock, working. It was time for me to go, and we would meet up later, I said. We both stepped outside the car. "You are spiritually connected," I said.

He grabbed me up for a hug and said, "We are connected!" I felt the divine covering us. We both reached for another hug before saying goodbye.

As I pulled away, I couldn't shake the feeling. I did not want to deal with the intensity of that energy again. It had been seven years. We had only had sex once, and I still felt the magnetic energy. We decided to meet later after I got off work, around nine.

I contacted my coworker and asked her if she could go out with me. I didn't know if the teacher was going to show up or not. We kept taking turns running from that type of energy. She was running late, and I was at the bar drinking wine. I felt him walking through the door. I turned around, and it was him. I started getting nervous because I could feel his energy when it traveled. I wanted to find out about that connection. I started nibbling on my chicken wings as I saw him approaching the seat. We both said our greetings. I stared at the sports bar TV because I did not want to look into his eyes. I felt him eyeing me from head to toe, as if I was not real and only in his imagination.

She popped around the corner with her daughter, and it was a relief because my heart was pounding. "Hey, girl, is someone sitting here?" She pointed to the other side of me. I looked surprised, as if I did not know she was coming.

He leaned over and whispered in my ear, "You invited your friend just in case I didn't show?" He smiled. How did he know how to read my thoughts?

He and my coworker were great at shooting pool. Her daughter and I sat back and talked while they played. I saw him for the first time at a distance. I stared at his figure. I did not know him in the 3-D form (body), but I felt like I knew his spirit (5-D) many lifetimes before. I wanted to hug, caress, and nurture him. He looked up toward my way, and I turned my face. He moved closer toward me, and I stood behind him, my arms wrapped all the way around his stomach. I rested the side of my face on his back.

My coworker noticed and said, "When did you start resting your face on a guy's back?"

"Leave her alone," he replied. She was drunk. I knew just in a few seconds she was going reveal everything before I had a chance to sit down and tell him. Was it possible he already knew?

She pointed her finger in my direction and said, "Well, missy, you better choose because you are in one hell of a mess."

I pointed toward a nice-looking guy that was muscular so she would let me handle my own business. She turned and said, "Oh my goodness." I chuckled because the guy was fine.

The teacher was over at the bar ordering drinks. I went in front of the pool table to get the cute guy's attention. I heard my coworker say, "You already have a guy here. Don't be blocking!"

I turned my hips to one side, raised my hand, and said, "Hello!" I could feel my speech getting a little off. I knew—no more wine for me!

"Oh Lord, she's drunk. Here she goes again," she yelled.

Then I saw another part of me looking at my body as a third person and saying, "The old life is over." I felt weird. My sexy self for men that served no purpose was gone forever.

He came back toward the seat. I danced on his lap. When I looked up, the guy that I was trying to tease motioned for me to come near. I could not move. I felt bound to that place. I turned to kiss his neck and laughed in his ear. "Have your fun! Soon it will be my turn to go toward your neck," he whispered. I jumped back.

It was two in the morning, time to leave. He and I walked outside. My coworker was behind, flirting. "Get in the car. It's cold," he said. I got in my car, and he stood outside of my car by the driver's door.

He looked cold as he stood there talking to me. He bent down toward the car window. Our lips came together in a kiss. As I breathed in, his breath went inside of mine during the kiss. When I breathed out, he sucked my breath into him during the exchange of a kiss. We kissed for at least twenty minutes. I looked at the clock, and it was already 2:45 a.m. He moved toward his car, and I gave him a wave because I did not know when I would see him again. He stared at me as he stood at his car. He waved his hands in a backward motion and said, "Just go," as he was trying to move the energy that kept coming toward him.

I walked in the front door to my home and noticed a text from him asking if I had made it home safely. I was feeling high off the energy. I did not respond to him and decided to let him know in the morning that I had made it home safely. Then I looked to the side and noticed I had another problem; it was my current partner. He grabbed his blanket and moved away from me where he was sleeping on the bed. I had forgotten I was living with him when I walked in.

When I was with the teacher, time stopped. There was no time or space between us, and it did not exist.

He started yelling at the top of his lungs, and it was the first time I saw him that angry. "You are careless! You do not care about anything!" he shouted. "You did not bother to call or text me when you were out." He was right. I had forgotten all about him. For the first time, I noticed I had no desire to argue or prove a point. I fell asleep, and it was a good one!

He went digging into my iPad and saw all my messages. There was no need for him to do that because I always reveal the truth. The next day, I told him about who I was with. I even showed him a picture of my coworker, the teacher, and myself that we took that night at the bar. I never had a desire to look through his phone, and I knew nothing about him. I knew deep in my heart there was no need to look for answers.

Later that week, I received a call from a coworker who said my current partner told an eighteen-year-old lady at our place of employment that we are not dating, and it was over. I wasn't mad because he was reflecting how I felt. However, I decided to ask him anyway. He told me he did that because of my texts with the teacher and the security guard. The guard and I occasionally met up. I felt it was time to meet up with him because I was proud he had become a police officer. I knew it was nothing more. Then he looked at me. "Why did you tell the teacher you miss sitting on his lap?" he asked.

"Because I do!" I replied. He kept quiet.

Flashback: I was sitting in the medical center working. I looked out the window. I wanted to go out in nature. I wasn't sure why at the time. It seemed to make me happy. I would release my worries, fears, and pain there. I ignored the feeling; it appeared to me in a dream. My brother and I were driving in a car. I was the driver. I wanted to get to work at the medical center, but I could not find my way. My brother turned to me and said, "Just log it into your GPS. We will get there."

We were in the middle of the desert. I put the address in my GPS, and it said, "Not found!" I thought, *Why would it say that? I work there.* I typed in the address again, and it said, "No location found!" I got out of the car and noticed it was not only a desert, but it was also the Grand Canyon. On the other side of where it split off was my dreams. It was a big gap. I woke up that morning trying to decipher it and prayed. I had a feeling that is was over with the job, but I proceeded to go to work anyway.

There was a nudge in my spirit that caused me to pull over. I rested at a park where there were a bunch of trees. For some reason, I looked at my inbox. There was an email from a spiritual master teacher. She said, "I know it seems as if your dreams are far away because of the Grand Canyon, but it is right there."

My heart started racing, and I closed my eyes. I could not start over again after that painful leap I took when I experienced great poverty. I noticed that was when I was unconsciously aware of my thoughts. This time, I knew the power of the mind and how it changed my life. I sat in the parking lot thinking about how I was going to go about the separation with employment.

It was ten minutes before my shift when I decided to start up the car. I drove in the direction of my job as I pondered the thought. I parked in the garage and got out of the car. I went inside the lab, and my coworker approached me and said, "You are not supposed to be here today."

I told her, "I know my schedule." She proceeded to look and called the manager.

I was at my desk and thought, *This is the third message in one day. She was right. I am not supposed to be here. My journey with them is over!*

She walked toward me and said, "The manager told you to report to another building."

I received the message, Lord, loud and clear! I went to my locker and got my belongings. There was another lady in the back. I was almost in tears when I said to her, "I want you to continue on the path of your school. Above all, follow your heart." I told her I would not be returning, and my time was up.

She hugged me and said, "You are such an inspiration." I walked out and got in my car. As I was driving off, my belly started to sweat, and I could feel water weight dropping off me as if I had just finished running. I wrote a letter to Human Resources to let them know about my departure from the organization.

My life started to change again. When I first met the guy from the C4 building, we saw 11:11 together. Then after that, I never saw it during the two years we spent in a relationship, with me working at the medical center.

I knew what I wanted. I wanted me and whatever else was connected when living in my truth. I looked up at a building and saw 1:11, and then every day I saw 2:22, 3:33, 4:44, 5:55, 616, 606,

2:02, and 2:12. All the numbers were moving quickly, and then it became clear to me.

I knew my truth. It was time for me to sit down and have a talk with my current partner. I recalled all my knowing and the experiences on my journey. Great cosmos connections that helped me get to know who I am. I told him, "I know who my twin flame is. It's been him all along." I looked at him and said, "I don't want to stop you from experiencing this great love. Love feels like the divine connection. You will have a sense of knowing. Your heart will tell you the truth."

He looked at me with confused eyes and said, "Okay." I wanted the Lord to confirm it for my conscious mind because my higher self knew all the answers.

I went to sleep that night and woke up around three in the morning. As I was sitting on the toilet, I started to pray because I had not seen the teacher that night in a dream, telling me the truth about us. I prayed and asked the Lord to reveal it. I went back to bed and had faith that he would.

I was in a dream state. I could still feel myself lying on my back in the dream. I could not move. My body was very still, and my arms were placed at my side. A download was transferring information to my conscious mind.

He had his left arm wrapped around me as he held me close to his chest. I rested my head where his heart was beating. He took his right hand and raised up my left arm. His index finger and thumb started to make a circle around my ring finger in the form of a band. I was aware I was dreaming. My mind received the message. I woke up thanking the Lord in my heart for revealing the truth. I felt the feeling of the teacher's presence beside me. Then I turned to the right side of the bed, and there was my partner sleeping.

Then I remember when God promised Sarah and Abraham a son in the Bible. Sarah was impatient, so she told her husband to sleep with the maid. That was not the promised son that God was telling them about. He blessed them anyway. I thought, *Did I try to create a false twin based on my knowledge and understanding? It was not a sense of knowing. How long have I ignored my heart?*

CHAPTER

18

Life Purpose

AFTER LEAVING THE LAB, I was already enrolled at a university. I had finished my semester off with a GPA of 2.90. I had to step back and analyze the situation. I was in the master's program as an information systems technician. I received a letter from the university in January saying I would be placed on academic probation if I did not pull up my GPA to 3.00 in the spring. I dreaded going into the database class. I wondered, *Why am I chasing degrees that do not fit into my personality and lifestyle?*

Then I realized I did it for the graduate school loan money, to make a transition toward a more fulfilling life. The grad loans were there to pay my bills. I only had on-call jobs. Tuesday, January 16, was when school would start back up. On the Friday before, I decided to take a leave of absence based on a gut feeling.

They approved it, and I was waiting for Tuesday because the twenty thousand was going to give me a comfortable living while

I found out what gifts were inside of me. Monday night, I had a dream of seeing 90999. I woke up trying to decipher it. I looked at my account and saw ten dollars and fifty cents instead of twenty thousand or the 90999 that I saw in my dream.

My heart was jumping out of my chest. It was rent time—plus car insurance, my car note, and other minor bills. I grabbed my laptop to look up my school account, and the twenty thousand was still sitting there. I phoned the school and found out the money transfers when you are taking active credit hours, and a leave of absence does not count.

I sat back and started to feel my heart. I knew something was happening. It was time. Of all the times I had asked God for a worldly job, it was time to stop playing around and step into my purpose. I sat on the edge of my bed. The number 90999 popped up in my head again. I grabbed my phone to decipher the meaning: *call to duty, humanitarian, lightworker, endings, and conclusions.* I laid my head back on my bed.

I remembered my daughter telling me about a Visa reward card. I applied for it before I knew this journey was going to shift my life. I got approved for a thousand dollars. It was enough to pay my half of the rent and car insurance. I was waiting for it to come in the mail. I walked outside of my front door and saw a court paper on my door for nonpayment of rent. I felt within me a feeling that said to trust the process. The date was for January 24, 2018. However, my Visa card came in the mail on January 22, and I was able to pay it before the court date.

I went in my room and lay down on the bed. *Here I go again with no job, not in school, and nothing to do.* I got a piece of paper and started studying my life. One the first day of writing, I wrote five thousand words, and it was flowing on paper as if my higher self knew all the answers. The next day, I went on writing. Then I recalled in the year when I was married—that was when I first started writing. Back then, I reached a hundred thousand words, and I trashed it! I realize I like to write, but I was still unconsciously aware of it.

I started writing again, and my higher self took over. I am the master of my life. My world around me is an illusion. I had to study and learn all my life challenges. Spending time in nature allowed me to open to my true self. It is the tree of life. It is my home where I belong.

Self-Reflection

As I reflect on my life and experiences, I cannot help but thank all the people who have crossed my path. I would like to speak about three topics: karmic mate, soul mates, and twin flame. Please remember to do your research, but this was my life experience, and I use self-help books and my intuition to help me decipher my journey.

Karmic Mates

So, let's get started! First, karmic mate. It is a haunting familiarity. If we have low self-esteem, then there is no escaping this one. It is our mirror of how we feel internally. My husband was my karmic mate. During my marriage, I played out my mom's vulnerable side, which was a part of myself that I denied. However, I acted out the male role most of my life. I forgave myself, my husband, and my father. That is when my life transformed from the karmic partner. I thank God for the experience and release.

Soul Mates

I encountered many soul mates on my journey and realized it is not just a romantic partner. It could be a mother, brother, father, friend, sister, or partner. Even though I encountered many, there were special ones who came across my path. One remembrance was my ex who passed away—may his soul rest in peace! We have a beautiful daughter. He was a man who loved the Lord and taught me about the great Jesus. My dad taught me about the great Allah. My mom was spiritually open to all greatness. I adapt to the philosophy of truth as of today! I am that I am, God, Cosmo, Spirit, Christ Consciousness; all of it resonates with me.

Another soul mate was my second daughter's dad. He taught me to open my heart to receive love and give love. He and I have an American Indian daughter who healed herself from a broken femur bone during meditation (no physical therapy) after the release from shock trauma. He and I are still soul friends but were once lovers.

This one soul mate at a club opened my route charka to sexual energy I never knew existed. With all other sex partners, I lived in my head, in my thoughts. I did not know what the feeling of sex in the base of my spine felt like until I met two lovers, a woman and a man to balance the yin and the yang within me. Yes, I had sex with a woman because I was adapting to the male energy in most of my relationships, out of fear and a desire to maintain control over my life after past hurts.

Accepting the female energy within my life kept my balance and gave back my female power. Now I am not saying we should sleep with a woman to get the yin back. It was my self-awareness when I became unbalanced, disowning a vulnerable part of myself. I will never forget her sexual energy, which gave me power to recognize my female energy.

Another soul mate was the security guard. I saw great potential in him. He was a security officer with dreams to become a police officer. He gave up hope and dropped out of college in the criminal justice field. I was angry at myself for not fulfilling my dreams (I had given up), but he showed up in my life as a mirror, and I hurt him with many words. He was also angry with me, and it was from his insecurities and fears. Two years after our separation, he became a police officer. I still met up with him to have occasional drinks, another connected soul friend of mine.

BJ, the Whole Foods guy, on the other hand, was dark energy that I was disowning. I always thought it was godly to be living in the light of righteousness. That did not work for me. I need to own up to all the dark and light energy within myself. I learned from him that I was not a victim of my circumstance and I should let it go. All the pain and the hurt and love again. He said he was suffering from me because I was cold as a turkey. We both were. When we got the message from each other, we moved on. We no longer have contact.

Another soul mate was the guy from the C4 building. He was the growing mirror of self- improvement. I love myself, and the reflection is showing up in my life as transformation. I see synchronicities everywhere. All universal numbers are appearing as 222, 333, 555, and 444, in addition to 1111.

Twin Flame

I left twin flame for last. We only have one in this lifetime. A twin flame is different from a soul mate (none are better than the other).

This person is the other half of your soul. It is you! Both of you split in half after reincarnation at the same time. Again, I am no expert. I am going on my life journey, metaphysical science (completion of a program), research, psychology, and my intuition. If it resonates with you, you will know.

When you see this person, you will recognize them. My experience was eye contact and a deep feeling and knowing in my inner self. We became friends. It is the fairy tale I was looking for as a child. But do fairy tales exist? This person is someone you will tell your dark secrets to, and you could never lie because they would know you are lying. All sins are confessed, left out in the open. When you are separate, you feel each other's hearts and telepathically read each other's thoughts. My experience was when my heart started to ache as if I had a heart attack, I knew he was thinking about me because I would see his face in my vision. Sometimes we would have a telepathic conversation while we were apart (speaking to each other's minds).

One day I was driving my car on the highway. In my vision, I saw the teacher under the hood of my car. He was checking my oil. I stood back and stared at him as I smiled. "Why are you smiling?" he said.

"I like looking at you," I replied. Then I jumped out of my vision. My focus went to the dashboard in my car. The engine light was on. I hurried up and got off the highway. When I got home, I checked my oil. It was bone dry. My car started to smoke. It was another message, and I had to put the pieces together.

Sorry to break the news to everyone. It is not the love of Romeo and Juliet! Beware this is a spiritual journey, a life purpose two people agree to. We will feel emotionally, mentally, and spiritually connected to the twin flame. My first experience was recognizing his voice. It is a free spirit connection. These two will not hurt each other. They are one, and there is no breaking free from this bond. They are in the fifth dimension. I tried for years to get this guy off my mind. The thoughts of him kept coming back. We are connected to the heart space forever.

When leaving earth, we will go home to another dimension together. Some twin flames decide to become romantic partners on earth while they complete their life mission together. However, it is not the purpose. The purpose is serving humanity. After the first meeting phase, during the enlightenment, one of the twins becomes the runner, and the other the chaser. I found out we were running from the inner clutter we had to clear, from false beliefs. Both are running from themselves. It is a process because of the issue at hand. I thought I was spiritually mature. I was not. He was my mirror of self-control. I had to learn to control my emotions.

What I wanted was in divine order. We both were afraid of this intense energy. I did not understand it at first. The old relationship on three dimensions is not working on earth. It has caused confusion, pain, and the need to control. I had to experience it in childhood and with other soul mates. The new paradox is the fifth dimension. We all will eventually become free spirits in the shift.

Our conversation through text would be a hi, hello, and good morning. Most people would view it as a third-dimension interaction, as if someone did not care or like them. He and I were (one of many twins) starting the source energy. Then it was another three years before we met again. Frequent thoughts would pop into our heads, and dreams would appear. During our first kiss, I saw in my vision a sacred union with this man as we breathed the breath of life into each other.

Our second meetup was at a social bar where I invited him. From my experience, these meetups are beyond our control, and we stayed away to balance out the energy. We both agreed to be best friends and lovers. We both are experiencing life challenges.

I want to make sure I am precise, and it is easy to decipher when I say twin flame. You will know because you will have a sense deep within your heart. Do not be obsessed with an unhealthy relationship with someone who chooses not to be with you.

Open your heart and let love guide you. Be free and live in your truth. The angels are here to guide us when asked. I love you all. We came to earth to experience, to learn, and to be free.

CHAPTER

19

Reprogramming My Mind

I HAD TO RELEASE years of negative thoughts. In doing so, I started reprogramming my mind. I was aware that 95 percent of our brain activity is operated off our unconscious mind (negative behaviors and thoughts). I did not trust men! However, we are only aware of 5 percent of our brain activity. It took me years to reprogram a new belief system. I wanted a life of meaning and a man that would be my best friend and lover. My old belief system was about controlling relationships and not about trust and honesty, because I was not honest with myself. I wanted to be free, so I had to set myself free. In return, my mirror was people reflecting to me areas in my life that I needed to improve.

In late 2012, working with adults with intellectual disabilities, I decided to start college in the human services field. I sat on my bed to think about the direction I was going to take to live a happier life. I heard within my gut (intuition), "As a man thinketh in his heart, so is he" (Proverbs 23:7). I read spiritual books on Buddha's teachings. I noticed when my chakras started to open, I could experience a fulfilling life for myself right here on earth—the life that I truly wanted. I took the knowing power I had and completed my associate of arts in human services management in 2015 at the University of Phoenix.

I continued college, completing my bachelor of health administration with a concentration in information systems. I graduated with honors. I was entering a new shift in consciousness, and when there were jobs that did not resonate with me, I did not stay. I was in it for the growing, learning, and experience! I started a second job at a medical center in 2015, resigning in 2017 after the completion of my bachelor's degree. It was an experience, but I wanted to help people cocreate a new life of relationships.

In 2017, I decide to go on call after many attempts of working full-time and part-time over a five-year period. I started to learn more about myself because it was my longest-held employment, and I decided to stay. Why was this? It was the job that paid less, but I found joy in human services. I got another job at a homeless prevention shelter in 2017. Sometimes I would only work three days in the month. My desire at the time was to move forward to graduate school. I applied only to one school at the time. I accepted the offer and entered grad school in the fall of 2017.

I was facing another challenge in my journey. I took a risk to live off $16,000 in grad loan money to meet my needs of sustaining a living. In the process, I discovered I am a writer. Where do I go from here? I do not know, but I am a cocreator of the universe. It is not only about thinking and speaking positive thoughts; it corresponds to our vibration frequencies. I firmly believe that, in the end, we are following our blueprint to our life path and higher calling. It is up to you. Will you answer the call?

CHAPTER

20

The Big Reveal

IN 2018, THE TEACHER invited me to watch him play basketball in the gym. It brought back memories because I grew up in that city. It was where we met at the school during my son's prekindergarten year. It was something he loved to do in his spare time.

He got out of the car. I could see him through the glass window of my vehicle. "Are you coming in or staying in the car?" he said.

"I will be in shortly," I answered. I watched him go inside, and I paced behind him. After eight years, the knowing was still there. I walked in and watched him play ball. He is a great ball player, but something had him out of it for a while.

He came over to where I was standing; he was out of breath. "I'm tired," he said. "I need to regain my strength." He started running around the gym and got down and did some push-ups. He walked back toward me.

"Just take little steps at a time. You will get there again," I said. "The point is you are still trying."

"Always," he said.

The game was over, and we both walked toward the car. "I want to get out of the school system," he said.

"You have been there your whole life. You are good with children," I stated.

"I want to start my own business. I just need to write a proposal."

My heart started racing because I love writing. What he did not know was I had left my jobs four months ago, doing on-call work to create a lifestyle of living. Out of faith, I was taking small steps. As he continued to talk, I noticed his strength was my weakness, and his weakness was my strength. He was good at saving money, and I was good at writing. At that point, I realized why I went to college. I learn a lot about writing a business proposal for health care. Another creative part of me came up after being back in contact with him again. On Valentine's Day, I sat in my room and wrote a poem. I handed it to him later that day after his basketball practice. It was time for the revealing.

The moment I knew was the day we kissed in the classroom.
Long ago but not forgotten!
I remember it like yesterday.
I just never knew the right words to say.

I ask myself,
Could you open to the possibilities you never knew?
Or will you secretly love at a
Distance?

But who are you to fool?

Everyone saw the words and laughter at the mention of his name.

What I saw was a listener, a friend, and a lover. I cannot pretend.

I listen very carefully to your words and concerns;

All I see are endless possibilities of a soul friend.

I pray the journey continues down the endless path,

Where we both find blissful endings ...

Trust and honesty are where I feel free,

And the treasures of my heart belong to you and me.

Happy Valentine's Day!

He went home that night, and he texted me, "I like that. Thank you! I like you, and like being with you," he said.

I remembered when he asked if he could have my heart. Back then, I laughed. It's not funny anymore. It takes vulnerability to share your heart openly with another person. "I want to spend the rest of my life with you," I said. "Do you want to get remarried and have any more children?" I asked.

"No more kids for me," he said. "Everything else is in God's plan. If time puts us in that place, I can go with marriage."

I thought, *I do not want any more children.* I felt a little disappointed about not receiving a straight answer regarding marriage. That is what it feels like to go with God's timing and a vulnerable part of myself that I have now accepted. He is learning to communicate. I am learning to be open and control my emotions. I let it go.

One thing I have noticed about a divine connection is that no matter how much one person runs, there is no need for the other to chase, because the universe has it covered in perfect timing. Will we stand side by side in partnership? One thing I am sure of is the intense energy moving me into my creative forces (life purpose) and trusting the universe. In God's timing.

My name is Cindy. I am a goddess. I came to earth to be a lightworker, to lift the vibration and consciousness of humanity. Everyone will awaken to the power within themselves. I am a metaphysics teacher and a graduate soul (twin flame) who has the power of vision and who receive messages in dreams and healing abilities. These are my gifts, and I use them in the co-creative process. I radiate life and enlightenment to the world, where we all are *one*. I am the divine.

Printed in the United States
By Bookmasters